you will rise

Sjana Elise Earp is an internationally renowned yoga instructor and a sunshine-seeking, hug-giving photographer, content creator, and adventure and travel enthusiast. She grew up on the east coast of Australia, where she spent much of her younger years channelling her abundant energy and curiosity into physical activities and her creative passions.

Having suffered from bullying, anxiety and depression, Sjana left school at age 16 when she gained early acceptance into university and began a degree in photojournalism. Gradually she started to embrace her favourite creative and physical pursuits again, sharing these and her journey of recovery on her Instagram page, @sjanaelise, where she now has 1.6 million followers from around the world.

Through yoga, travel, photography and writing, Sjana has rediscovered a love and compassion for herself and everything around her. She is a staunch advocate for self-acceptance and body confidence, mental health, equality and the environment. Now, Sjana finds bliss by sharing her passion for life with the world, and encourages everyone to find and shine their own inner light, too.

you will rise

SEEK, SOOTHE AND SOAR

SJANA ELISE EARP

EBURY
PRESS

Contents

To my reader

It may sound hella hippie, but before we begin, I invite you to close your eyes, place your hands over your heartbeat, and take three long, slow breaths.

Connect your mind to your body, and your body to your breath.

Slow down, soften and find a sense of stillness.

Go ahead, I'll wait.

Give your inner self permission to feel. To feel abundantly, unapologetically and without judgement.

Your emotions have a voice. Listen.

Your feelings are valid.

You are valid.

My prayer is that these pages may serve as your emotional bible. A handbook for the hurt and for healing. A place you can come to, and come back to, as often as you like, for a gentle reminder of the light not only around you, but also the light within.

May these words illuminate your internal landscape, and ignite a glow of guidance and gratitude as you move closer to your own truth.

For the light seekers and the love givers. This one is for you.

For anyone who has ever loved and lost. This one is for you.

For the sensitive souls, the magic makers, the time takers. This one is for you.

I firmly believe that everything happens for a reason. So chances are, if you are reading these words, you have been drawn here for a purpose.

This isn't a coincidence, it's divine timing — the cosmos aligning perfectly, as it always does.

You are meant to be here.

Why?

Because you're here.

These words were not easy for me to write.

In fact, I have been writing them for the past seven years.

This book is an honest reflection of all my past selves. It's the story of my evolution.

A recollection of my countless rebirths. A memoir of both my miracles, and my mistakes.

These pages are lined with all of the conversations I've had with the moon.

It is a book of memories: my path of growth, heartbreak, love, expansion, loss, healing, manifestation and divine surrender.

I can look at any one of these poems, and remember exactly where I was when I wrote it, who it is about, and why I wrote it.

These words are not just a collection of curated poems and phrases, they are my written vulnerabilities. Some of my biggest secrets, greatest losses and most memorable moments are etched into the space between your palms right now. And I don't know whether to be proud or terrified — or both.

Refer to this book as I do the ocean. You may feel called to dive right in, to fully submerge yourself. Or perhaps you'll prefer to just dip your toes in every now and then.

I sometimes like to close my eyes and flick the pages until my intuition tells me to stop.

I always find that whatever I open to is what I need to hear most that day. Perhaps you'll like to do the same.

I hope this is the kind of book that you can come back to at different stages of your life, and see or learn something new about your own self each time.

Whatever this book makes you feel, whatever it ignites or unearths, I hope you can find self-compassion and understanding. May it support you, and reassure you that it takes immense strength to remain soft in a world of concrete structures and beliefs.

My hope is that you give yourself permission to truly *feel*.

Without judgement, without trying to understand or comprehend. Just feeling wholeheartedly, and unapologetically.

May this book brighten your shadows, illuminate your path and walk you home to yourself.

From my heart to yours.

Sjana x

Unfold
& Unearth

Plant yourself. Dig your roots into the earth, allow her to nourish

you, and give yourself space to grow.

Bloom.

Unfurl, blossom, open.

Don't shy away from the sun.

Instead, make its light your own.

Shine, darling.

Just as you were intended.

Sister,
You. Are.
Significant.

Your visions will continue to manifest in direct proportion

to the amount of courage that resides within your heart.

There is a rhythm. Bringing harmony into life. You are magic in
    motion.

You are divine chaos; a blazing wildfire.

You're a whirlwind of emotions.

You're a threatening tornado and a silken sunflower, all at once.

You're like an earthbound rainbow, coloured-in curves.

Bent but not broken, shaped by the ways of the world.

You're a grain of sand, and the entire ocean.

You're made of sunlight and moon dust.

You're capable of hurting and healing; swimming and sinking;
    floating or flailing.

Failure whispers, but you persevere.

Driven by passion, moved by the echoes of your mind.

Haunted by love, helped by music and touched only by those
    worthy of tasting their sins.

May you live with wonder, not worry. Curiosity, not caution.

Moments aren't made of minutes; they're made of opportunities.

Whether or not you choose to utilise these opportunities,

is entirely up to you.

Continue to fall in love with the process of unravelling.

Disentangle your mind, unwind your soul and unknot the kinks
in your heart.

Undo all the ropes you've wound so tightly around yourself.

The shackles that have held you, suppressed you and imprisoned
you.

Release the thoughts, and the stories you tell yourself.

Breathe through the resistance, the urge to fall effortlessly back
into your old self-sabotaging behaviours, and instead open
your arms and heart to the possibility of radical growth and
complete love, contentment and acceptance of your soul
and the body that holds it.

Open wide to unearth your purest and truest self.

One day, you'll look back and remember this moment, this
decision, as the place where it all began.

I've always found trees fascinating.

The way they are equally as valuable, equally as intricate and equally
as beautiful below the surface, as they are above.

The branches reaping the praise for bearing fruit, when the roots
do all the hard work.

What parts of you are buried? How can you give those parts light?

What fruit are you growing? Is it healthy?

Where are your roots planted? What makes you feel humbled,
grounded and connected to the earth?

Is there anything else you could do today to help you recognise and
feel your inner growth?

Anything you could do to help you bloom?

Have the courage to pay attention to your body. It has an innate

ability, a natural intelligence — an unwavering brilliance.

The deepest of insight and understanding, an extraordinary

acumen.

It is constantly providing you with subtle cues;

Your body knows what it needs.

All you need to do is listen.

Give yourself the gift of listening to your body, and having the

courage to respect it.

And sometimes you just need to respect your heart, remove yourself from the situation and walk barefoot in nature until you can breathe again.

Find who you are. Find who you are without relying on anyone or anything else. Find comfort in your own existence, and an honest acceptance of your own being.

Once you are entirely certain and proud of your own person, there isn't much you cannot do. You'll see.

The illumination of my light,

does not reduce the brightness of yours.

A star need not destroy other stars to be seen.

I'm human.

I'm flawed and faulted

My seams are split, and

corners are curved

I'm bent, but not yet broken.

My phases change like that of the moon

And it is because of her,

I know I'll rise again.

And again.

Darling, your
soul isn't lost.
It's just extremely
adventurous.

Whatever you think you are, you are not. You simply are.

Hey you,

Friendly reminder that you're a powerful, angelic and
    extraordinary being.

Your existence is meaningful.

You have a purpose designed by fate herself.

And you are exactly where you are supposed to be.

So breathe.

Breathe, sit back, and enjoy this glorious mess we call life!

Whatever you do, do it with your whole heart. Do it with your whole soul. Do it with meaning. Do it with intention. Do it with grace. Do it with lightness and do it with love. Do it with thought. Do it with compassion and do it with kindness.

And sometimes you'll be too much woman for him to handle.

I can tell you with complete certainty that this is your power, not
your poison.

For being female means that our vulnerabilities are also some of
our greatest strengths . . .

Our passion, our curiosity, our empathy, our compassion, our
emotions, our instincts, our ability to be bossy and demand
the attention of any room we choose.

We are women.

We're sassy, sensitive and divinely feminine.

We are light beings — infinite beauty; walking, talking mysteries.

We are the mothers, the daughters, the sisters, the lovers, the
leaders. The friends, the neighbours, the teachers,
the learners. We are divine creatures, made of the same
starshine and moon dust that fill the sky. Crafted by
Mother Nature herself.

We play beneath the sun and move with the tides.

Our bodies are miracles, and our minds are magic.

We are W O M E N.

Worthy Of More Equality Now.

Suppressing sensation is not my desire.

Being vulnerable doesn't make me weak.

It makes me wonderfully and wildly human.

So at times, I'll be erratic.

At times, I'll be irrational.

I'll be unpredictable and stubborn and rigid.

Because I have the ability to feel, and I plan on practising my right

to do so.

Every day I'm stepping closer and closer towards my true self.

I can feel it; all the internal shifts and reshaping.

Each day I re-learn my potential as I re-realise my strengths.

Every new moment I breathe life in to acknowledge the depth of

     my feminine nature, and release control to surrender to the

     spirit within.

53

Life doesn't have to be stressful, chaotic and rushed.

Take a step back, let the breeze brush your hair.

Take a deep breath, submerge yourself in the ocean's molasses.

Relax, allow your cells to rest.

Stop, appreciate your surroundings.

Look up, admire the vastness of nature.

Look down, notice the earth beneath your feet or the sand between
your toes.

This world is wild and wonderful.

It is meant to be fulfilling, inspiring and entirely unforgettable.

Moments are supposed to be experienced with your whole
being; body, mind, soul, spirit, intuition and all of your
senses.

You are allowed to find contentment, happiness and love.

You are worthy of living an extraordinary life.

Allow your joy,
To be your healing.

You are nature herself.

Pure and raw beauty. You are embodied divinity, a Goddess of

goodness and grace.

Be gentle with your soul, dear one, for she too is growing. Honour

her expansion, honour her transformation.

Be accepting and forgiving. Water the roots of change, and watch

in awe as you sprout seedlings of self-love, and rise in your

own light.

And all this time, I was searching for something that was already

buried within me.

Sweet dear,

This body is not your enemy.

I need you to know that it is safe to be imperfect.

Safe to unfold, unlearn and unearth.

We are like kaleidoscopes, infinitely changing forms.

— Human kaleidoscope

You'll know her when you see her.

She's the one with unbrushed hair, sunkissed skin, socks that don't match, restless feet and a smile from ear to ear.

I'm consciously detaching myself from the material world.

Removing, recycling, reducing.

The things I own, the things I cling to and the emotions and beliefs
I wear so heavily.

I know my worth is not measured by possession. My value is not
determined by anything exterior to my heart, nor has it ever
been.

We have all been dearly gifted with everything we will ever need.
Source herself provides an infinite abundance of wealth,
health and miracles.

Remembering this has been a portal to unearthing my magic, and
a catalyst to witnessing my immeasurable potential.

To whoever you are, and wherever you may be.

If you are reading this, I hope you have an extraordinary day.

I hope you have great insight and knowledge. I hope you feel
grateful and whole. I hope you see greatness and hope.
I hope you find contentment and happiness in the things
you do, the people you're surrounded by and are able to
recognise the countless miracles that occur throughout
each and every moment.

I hope you know you are loved.

I hope you know you are capable and strong and powerful beyond
measure.

I hope you feel as fabulous as you truly are.

You deserve nothing short of extraordinary moments and a divine
life experience.

Discipline is not giving up on yourself.

It is finding determination, even in failure.

Discipline means 'I trust in myself, and I won't give up.

I trust in myself. And I trust in the things I am doing.'

Discipline = consonance.

Balance is a fine dance in life.

And as a woman, I am a contrast of extremes: hard and soft, strong
yet sensitive, hot and cold, emotional and analytical.

Within me, I have both masculine and feminine energy, pulsating
throughout my being. Both ends of the spectrum aiding me
equally. Understanding this is the first step. Acknowledging
it is the second. And learning to truly embrace it, without
fear or judgement, is how one comes to cultivate a life of
contentment.

I am ready.

I'm ready for the good, and the bad that comes today. I am ready to
fight if needed, and to surrender when necessary. I am ready
to push through, jump over, hurdle, run and stride with
confidence and purpose. I am ready to muster up courage,
to be the strength I need and to overcome anything that is
thrown in my direction.

I am ready to kill with kindness, to feel immensely and to live
wholeheartedly.

Today, I am ready.

Repeat after me:

'The only thing holding me back from stepping into my truth,

    is me.

I am my own obstacle.

I have chosen to listen to the doubt, to the fear. I have enabled it to

    dictate my direction.

I have unintentionally been giving power to the tales I have told.

I now consciously choose to release the stories I used to tell myself,

And choose to grow through these lessons.

My trials will serve as tools toward my triumphs.

My feelings will pave the way for my healing. And today, this

    moment, will be the beginning of something, some*one*,

    wonderful.'

It is safe to shine,

To be wildly uninhibited.

It is your time to be fiercely feminine,

No longer a stranger to the strange.

Embrace your duality,

Embody every unique phase with grace and curiosity.

Bow down to your own transitory nature,

Worship the ethereal Goddess within.

For you are nature herself.

You are the deepest oceans and all of her creatures.

You are the snow-capped mountains, and the echoing valleys in
   between.

You are the red dirt canyons, the gushing creeks that transform
   into breathtaking waterfalls.

You are the dense forest floors, and the majestic songs this world
   so sweetly sings.

You are the beautiful silence at 5am,

The pink that paints the skies, the dew that dances on grass and the
   intricate webs that glisten in the sunlight.

Give yourself permission to be every bit of woman you were
   destined to be.

Then bloom, baby.

Bloom, bloom, *bloom*.

Love
& Lust

All that exists is love.

Love, in limitless forms.

Love, in countless colours.

Love, in infinite abundance.

We humans, we are shaped by genetics, environments, people, knowledge, values, experiences, and most of all we are shaped by what we love.

And you deserve someone who is willing to endure that possibility,

    just to see your face each morning.

You deserve the kind of love that is so intense it scares those

    around you.

The kind of love that is so overwhelming it's a miracle your body

    can even hold it, that your mind can even fathom it.

You deserve a love beyond comprehension.

Understanding > Desire

Forget chemistry, search for CONNECTION.

Find your fellow light beings. Immerse yourself in the
infectious energy they exude. Dance to the vibration you
share. Submerge in a higher frequency and give without
expectation. When you find your tribe, your people, your
person — your twin flame, your soulmate, your sunshine —
love them unapologetically, love them unconditionally,
love them without boundaries or limits. Love them freely,
honestly, wonderfully. Love them infinitely, without
reservation or fear.

Love them without judgement, love them with nothing but honesty
and vulnerability.

Love them wholeheartedly, knowing that in doing so you are
willingly giving them the power to break you, but trusting
that they won't.

I don't want a wanderlust — I want a wanderlove. Intimate, overwhelming, passionate and indescribable.

I just need to be touched.

I need to be held, kissed, caressed.

I need someone to tell me their secrets and share their stories.

I need someone to admit their flaws and vulnerabilities to me.

To bloom in my presence and grow by my side.

And to be okay when I unravel by theirs.

I need the intimacy, the passion.

I need the warmth of a growing love, endless tomorrows and the

possibility of forever.

Find the one who makes you better,

The one who sets your soul on fire.

Find the one who makes you smile until your cheeks hurt,

And laugh until your tummy cramps.

Find the one who you can be raw with; whether it be 9pm skinny
dips, midnight cuddles or 3am conversations about the
universe.

Find the person you want to be with through thick and thin, rain,
hail or shine.

The person you think of when you're trying not to think of
anything.

The person you find yourself smiling about whilst doing
something boring.

Find your human, your kindred spirit and intertwine your souls
together like growing vines.

Not because you need to own them or become anything in
particular, but because life without them in it isn't quite so
colourful and bright.

Find your sunshine, and bask in their warmth simply because it
feels good.

Don't try to change them. Just immerse yourself in their existence

and adore them for whatever and whoever they are.

Love them, unconditionally.

And let them love you too.

Open up that dusty door and enjoy the feeling of happiness filling

your heart once more.

Trust fate, trust the Universe.

Take ten seconds of insane courage and a couple of deep breaths

and understand that everything happens for a reason.

Stop questioning. Remove your doubt and flow with the sorcery

this life has so kindly given you.

Sometimes things can feel right, simply because they are. No

hidden agenda, no traps, just life and all of its wonderful

mysteries uncurling like a flower in the spring.

Blossom, baby.

Let it grow. Let it be exactly what it is intended to become.

Destiny has a funny way of manifesting itself.

Sure, it could end miserably.

Or, this could be the start of a thousand little eternities sewn

together by universal truths and intentions.

My soul collided with yours and that was it.

That was the end of everything as I knew it.

And just the beginning of everything else.

97

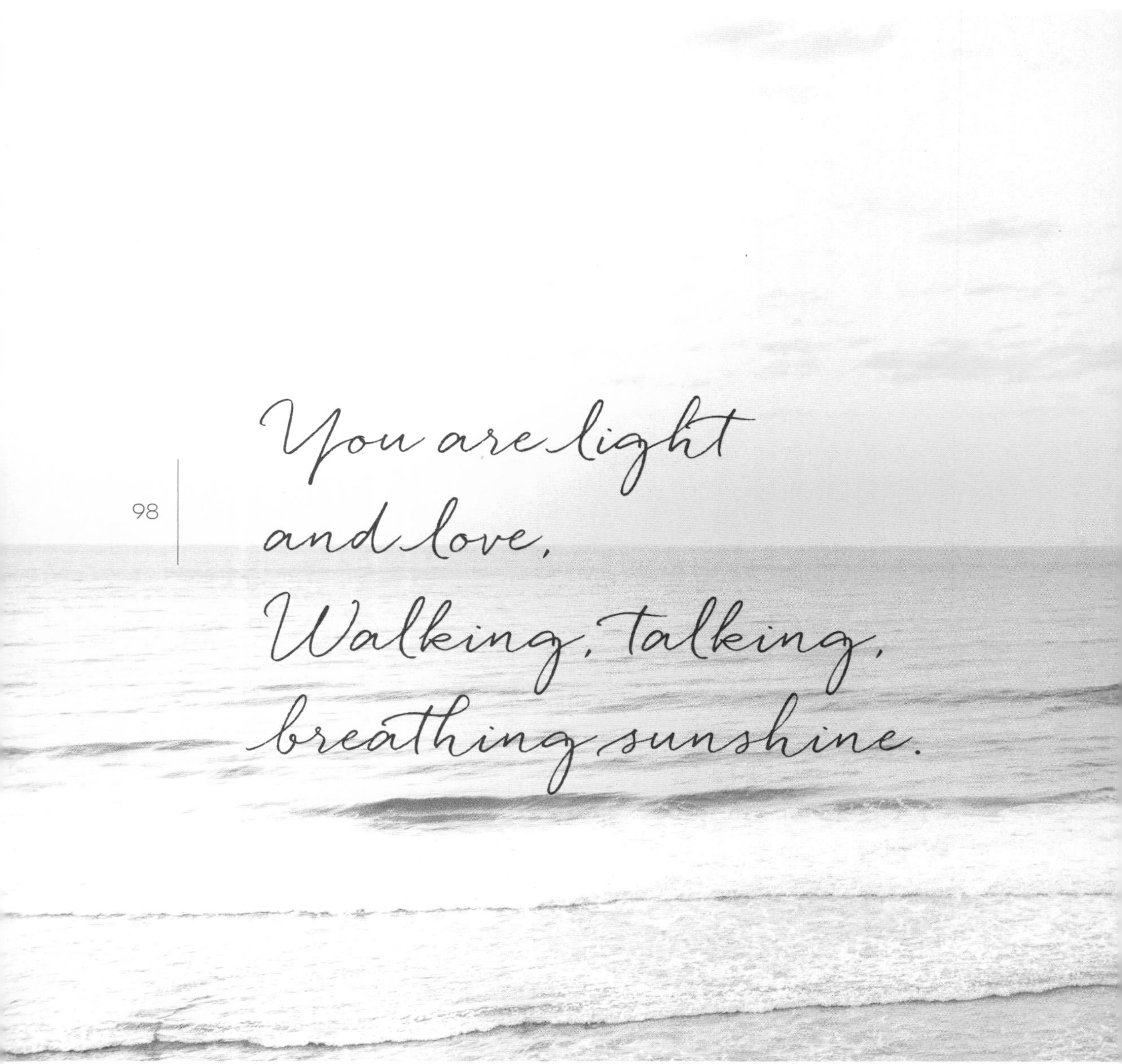

You are light
and love,
Walking, talking,
breathing sunshine.

I fell in love last night

I fell in love, all over again.

Uncontrollably, irrationally

I didn't want to, but inevitably I did

It was the way he kissed me,

I think

Sweet and soft; delicately

Cautiously, carefully

The way a child holds a newborn.

He'd run his thumb gently across my lips adoringly

Then hold my flushed cheeks in his palms,

As if he was holding the future.

Skin to skin,

I could feel his warm breath heating the air between our lips

He smiled

And I melted.

Perhaps it was the way our bodies curved together

Intimate;

Perfectly parallel

If lines could sing, we were a perfect harmony.

Or maybe it was the way he planted kisses

Like seeds along my spine and shoulders

He traced maps

With his fingertips

Across my skin.

He wouldn't let me go.

And I didn't want him to.

I wanted to stay in his arms

Pressed against his body, forever.

He makes me feel infinite,

Cosmic.

He and I together, is as if

The moon and stars collide.

An indescribable explosion

Capable of shifting time.

Him: I wanted to know which way you would guide me.

Her: Towards love! Always towards love!

The possibility of a lifetime of magic will always outweigh the

possibility of heartbreak.

Don't hold back in any affair where the heart is concerned.

A luminescent love.

A connection that light pours into, and curls up inside of.

An explosion of cosmic energy.

A collision of divinities.

A creator of destinies.

A space where growth manifests,

and life blooms.

Sometimes, people have stars inside them.

And other times, people are the stars.

And the moons.

And all their galaxies.

They're worlds of wonder and intrigue.

They're oceans of colour and energy and their hearts are warmer

than the sum of all the suns.

They're pure light, overflowing with love.

Complicated creatures simplified by a human shell.

A hardened exterior.

Countless cells creating intricate and fragile systems.

An existence as complex as the cosmos.

You're no accident.

Baby, you're nothing short of a miracle.

When I wake up in the morning,

I don't need coffee.

It's you I crave.

You smell like homemade pancakes,

And taste like sugar syrup.

Warm like tea,

Smooth like cream.

Breakfast all day, every day.

You were the stranger I recognised.

The light through the dark.

And it was within the corners of your existence,

I also recognised myself.

My favourite place
is the space between
your arms.

His touch is such a magical thing.

The way a single fingertip gliding across my skin can control me.

Losing all inhibition.

Skin to skin, the heat penetrates my bones. Milk and honey. I melt
like butter.

He tastes like strawberries. Even in the morning, it tickles my lips
and invigorates my soul.

His hands on me, moving across my body like waves.

Covering me with his warmth.

His scent dances around the room and fills my nostrils. He smells
like vanilla ice cream on a hot summer's day. A scent that
reminds me of childhood, and happiness.

A scent that reminds me of home.

His breath, heating my neck, sends chills down my limbs.

I close my eyes and try not to float away.

This feeling. Him. Us.

It's the genesis and resolution of everything.

If I shall wander,

Pull me closer.

Loop your rope around my heart,

And paint your art across my limbs.

Merge your skin with mine,

As we interlace our souls.

Fish me from the sea of my own evil,

And back towards your light.

For I am yours,

Now and for eternity.

'You won't be able to hold her back,' he said.

'She's like an erratic butterfly, or the unforgiving tide.

She is euphoric, tantalising and whimsical.

She'll tease your senses — but you'll never be able to hold her, for
     she never stops.

She's the anticipation before a first kiss, she's the sound of soft rain
     on your roof at night.

She is freshly picked daisies and the pastel glow of pinks in the
     morning sky.' He smiled as he glanced down and aimlessly
     stirred his lukewarm coffee.

'She's crazy, uncontrollable, irrational, spontaneous,
     unreasonable and illogical.

She's disorganised, indecisive, kooky, mad and entirely ridiculous.

Yet I'm absolutely, well and truly, 100 per cent, hand on heart,
     head over heels in love with her.'

Home.

They say home isn't a place; it's a feeling.

And it's a beautiful concept. To define home not by a postcode,
    but instead by the sense of belonging you can find through
    a passion, a purpose or a person.

And I would always agree with the concept, longing to believe with
    my heart not my ears.

It wasn't until I met you that I truly felt the evidential truth.

The thing, though, is that I didn't find my home within you.

I found my home within me, because of you.

But I like that you've moved in.

Creased cloth drapes from earth-kissed limbs, teacups stained
    with traces of yesterday.
His caffeine kisses linger on my lips whilst his fingers trace my
    hips.

When you speak
I hear oceans.
The ocean has always
been my favourite
place to be.

He kissed me like I was made of magic.

And I guess for a second, I was.

I love you.

There. I said it.

And I'm not afraid to say it again!

I love you, I love you, I love you!

I love you when you wake up. I love you when you fall asleep.

I love you when you dream. And I love you every moment
in between.

Love comes in,
The tide goes out.
Move with the waves,
No fear or doubt.

The turbulence; the push, the pull.

The mystery, the unknown.

It's red, dangerous.

I need to submerge.

Cool and salty

Waves washing me clean,

Crashing whitewash purifying tip to toe.

Hair tugs and salty kisses of a different kind.

The longing burns.

Again, I'm trying to bite my teeth.

The roundabout with no exit.

The room with no door.

Familiar.

I smell the storm.

I hear it roar.

The moisture weakens a scream.

Look in my eyes;

Those aren't stars, they're endless galaxies.

Deeper than an ocean.

The further you go, the less you will see.

You kissed me.

Threw me against the doorframe and held my face in your palms.

You kissed me deeply, passionately.

And then moved your hands across my body as if you were

     decoding braille.

Sure, it was a little awkward,

A little flimsy,

And a lot like a first time.

Because it was a first time.

The first of many.

The first of moments and magic.

The first of laughter and lifetimes.

And I wanted it to be the first of everything.

I wanted *you* to be the first of everything.

That wasn't the problem.

The problem was that I wanted you to be the last of everything, too.

It's amazing that a heart can shatter completely,

And yet the world won't skip a beat.

I miss affection;

Lips on my neck,

bruises on my hips,

his hot breath between the curves of my legs.

The merging of flesh,

the unity of breath,

the entanglement of limbs,

the ecstasy of release.

The past is cruel.
I feel like a fool,
For loving you.

Our love was like a wildfire.

Lit in ecstasy, ignited with passion, and fueled by dream-like
illusion.

Easy to start, quick to spread, rampant and unpredictable.

Then all-consuming, relentless, devastating.

I thank you for my destruction, as it is from these same ashes that
I will be reborn.

For the same nature that heals a forest, is inside of me.

Against all odds, I will grow through this darkened dust,
and thrive once more.

I just need someone to love me. And I need that someone to be myself.

Seduce your
own soul.
Touch her
in every way,
every day.

I am continuously falling in love with the process of becoming

myself.

149

A wise man once told me to repeat these words out loud, every

      morning when I wake up:

I love my life.

I love life.

I love.

Love.

Accept
& Surrender

You are already exactly where you are meant to be. You already

hold all the power you need, and you are already capable

of finding and feeling true happiness and fulfilment.

All the tools you need to create the life you desire, are

already within you.

You are not broken. You are not missing pieces, flawed or lost.

You are a whole, strong, capable, intelligent, beautiful being.

In order to access your true and highest power, all you need to do is

believe you are enough.

From now on, I'm saying 'YES'.

Yes to the things that I was once afraid of. Yes to the things beyond
my comfort zone. And yes to everything I used to say no to.

Yes to me. Yes to you.

Yes to liberation. Yes to healing. Yes to expansion.

Yes to LOVE.

Forgive yourself.
Acknowledge
yourself.
Embrace your truth.
Breathe.

I used to think control was power.

I was wrong. Control isn't power. It's the opposite. Power is the
ability to let go. To be flexible. To find contentment even
when we have no control. To find balance when life is chaotic
and erratic. To accept and welcome, with open arms, the
inevitability of change and unpredictability.

Power is the ability to be powerless and still find the strength to be
hopeful, happy and wholesome.

Life isn't about being (or appearing to be) perfect.

Life is about the freedom of expression, the right to be silly, and being wonderfully adventurous.

Life is about making friends with unexpected people, following your heart and dancing to the beat of your soul.

Life is about doing the things that make you feel vibrant, colourful and energised.

Watching the sunrise, doing spontaneous things, getting amongst nature, soaking up the sunshine and inhaling fresh air, dipping your toes in the ocean or finding a new place to lose yourself for a couple of hours.

You don't have to achieve or be anything in particular.

All you need to do is exist.

Just be.

It really is that simple.

Open your heart.

Surrender.

In each new moment, ask yourself,

'Does this move me closer to living in alignment with my truth?'

'Does this make me more centred in love?'

'Is this a decision I am making out of abundance? Or fear?'

React accordingly.

Seek refuge within your breath,

Acknowledge the steady beating of your heart,

Feel it knocking on the door to your chest,

And know that you are always home.

Be gentle on yourself, darling. You don't need to be hard and bold against the world. It is okay to sink, surrender and soften. Melt and merge back to the earth, unfold and embrace the opportunity for ecstatic rebirth.

And like the ocean, her heart sways to the beat of something

    greater.

Rising and falling,

Coming and going.

The flow of life.

Pushed and pulled by the tugs of love; a spontaneous occurrence,

    an accidental scenario, or a change of mind.

A red light, a broken clock, a slow train, a missed bus, a talkative

    stranger, a wrong turn. Insignificant coincidences — destiny

    and life colliding in perfect harmony.

Thank you. I see you. I love you.

My most honest reflection.

My brightest light.

My best friend.

My soulmate.

—A poem about me. A poem about you.

Sometimes you'll feel inferior.

You'll feel small and insignificant.

Belittled and irrelevant.

Don't allow this to bury you.

Don't allow it to weigh on you.

Instead, let it be a time to recognise how vast this world is. How
your existence is but one aspect of this infinitely expanding
Universe. Look at the mark you leave on this world; walk
along the beach and see your footsteps trailing behind you.

Stop, and watch as the ocean devours any evidence of your
existence.

You can choose to allow this to consume you. Or you can bask in
the awe of the almighty and surrender yourself to a more
powerful source.

We are but a drop in a sea; one star in the galaxy; one petal in a
field of flowers.

Allow that thought to be warming, comforting. Allow that concept
to fill you with immense satisfaction and contentment.

Your shadows
hold beauty too.

What matters most, is the relationship you have with yourself.

It's about the words your lips don't speak, the thoughts that float

atop the ocean in your mind, and the clumsy dance between

your heart and soul.

Don't stress, don't stir. Just sit, and allow the magic to happen in its own time.

Breathe. Step back. And laugh at the idea of consistency.

Because maybe your life isn't predictable. Maybe you have been
zigzagging across the board your entire existence; stopping
and starting here, there and everywhere. And that's okay. As
long as you are always moving, always chasing something and
always challenging yourself, then you're doing just fine.

You will always end up *exactly* where you need to be.

You are your home.

Your heartbeat.

Your skin.

Your mind.

You are the only person you will ever need.

And when you no longer expect this world or another soul to set

your own free, you'll automatically find the liberation you

seek.

Feel what you need to feel.

And feel it completely.

Then, let it go.

Listen to the Universe,
and allow its songs
to silence the mind.

Emotions don't have words.

Words, we give later.

Emotions are just guests,

and you are the host.

I will give more
than I take.

Dear girls,

You are not flawed. You are a wild and wonderful existence.

You are a miracle.

You are an artwork of nature; divine and intricate — the epitome of
unique beauty.

You're rare and raw, a special kind of complex.

You do not need to alter yourself to merge into a mould. Your
untamed edges are fringed with all things lovely. You're
laced with an angelic aura. Your natural state is deific;
a combination of the human and the Divine.

There is nothing about you that is not perfectly imperfect. You
are designed to be this way; superlative. If someone is not
able to recognise your worth, this is a reflection of them —
not you. Your value is measured in magic and your ability
to transform the lives of those around you. Your value is
measured by your ability to make others smile and light up

any room you enter. Your value is measured in goodness and grace; kindness and compassion. Not the width of your waist or the amount of air between your thighs.

You are an enchantress of happiness and light. You seduce life itself.

Your body curves like ocean waves and you move like water itself.

You are an English rose, a French kiss, a warm hug and a pastel sunrise. You are a floating butterfly, a flower in spring, a 2am conversation and the moon you dance beneath. Your existence is intended to be impassioned, illustrious and brilliant.

You are all things luminous and light.

I hope one day, you can see that for yourself.

Remove resistance
and succumb to the
destiny outlined in
the stars.

Being naked has nothing to do with the amount of clothes you
wear.

Real nudity = real vulnerability.

To anyone who needs to hear it . . .

This is for you.

For those of you who feel isolated, distanced, lonely.

For those of you who can't remember how to smile.

Or laugh.

For those of you who don't think anyone else will understand.

For those of you who feel pathetic, worthless, useless . . .

Or worse, completely numb.

You are loved. YOU ARE LOVED.

I know you hate yourself and think that this feeling will last forever.

I know.

I know you're hurting, longing, waiting. I know you feel like the
storm won't pass.

I know.

I know that you have no motivation, no energy, and you don't
see the point of anything. I know your every thought is
controlled by something dark and sinister.

I know. I know how much you wake up wishing you hadn't.

I know what it feels like to hate yourself that much.

I know.

I know you think you'll never remember what happiness feels like,
and that you think it will never get any better.

I know. But I also know that it will.

It will get better. And you will feel happiness again.

I know that there is so much to look forward to in life, and these thoughts and feelings are only temporary.

I know you will smile again, and laugh so hard milk runs out of your nose. I know you'll feel love, try new things, travel to far-off places, and taste foods you didn't know existed.

I know you'll overcome this battle. And countless others.

I know you'll live a full life of mistakes but hold no regrets.

I know you'll feel the sand between your toes again, again experience many more first kisses and probably lose your clothes when you go skinny dipping.

I know you'll probably take endless photos, trek mountains, and make memories you couldn't even dream of.

I know you'll probably have your heart broken, maybe more than once . . .

But then you'll be okay again. Because I know you're strong.

Because you've lived with yourself, for just another hour, or just another day, when all you wanted to do was stop existing.

That's the hardest thing you'll ever have to do.

And you're already doing it . . .

I know it's worth it.

I know. You are loved.

We all have things we need to let go of.

To combat negativity:

1. Become witness; don't suppress. Don't express. Just watch.

2. Repeat 1.

There is a great strength to be harnessed,

In admitting your vulnerability.

There is no next,
only this.
There is no then,
only now.

Place one hand on your heart, and the other on your belly. Feel the
      rise and fall of your breath; movement of the energy within.
Know that you are home.
You are home.
You are home.
You are *home*.
The work is done. Now is the time to rejoice, surrender and
      remember.

Growth & Gratitude

Here's to change — to motivation transforming into an unrivalled determination, and the urgency of goodness and wellness conquering all forms of negativity.

Here's to hope.

Here's to new beginnings.

Here's to walking away from excuses.

Here's to welcoming a challenge with an open mind.

Here's to ridding ourselves of self-doubt.

Here's to striving to better ourselves, regardless of external opinions.

Here's to strong people, with even stronger minds.

Here's to eagerness for greatness.

Here's to unexpected inspiration.

Here's to thanking the people who support us, for encouraging and reassuring us in moments of need.

And here's to thanking the people who don't support us, for pushing us just that little bit harder.

This is my pledge, my promise for change.

Not for the approval, praise or respect of others, but for the love and acceptance of myself.

Some days aren't filled with rainbows and postcard-worthy sunsets. Some days you don't achieve the things you set out to and the road steers you off your path. Detours happen. Surprises exist. Unfortunate things occur. Life with all its glory is inevitable — it will happen whether or not you want it to, whether or not you are ready for it and regardless of your preparation (or lack of). But these misfortunes are often blessings in disguise.

These obstacles and challenges tend to be miracles; messages from higher vibrations sent directly to us with purpose. Sent to us with the intention of growth, positive transformation and triumph.

The strongest people I know have been shaped by the hardest experiences.

The best things in life are free.

Ocean dips, salt drying on your skin, a friendly smile, the feeling of grinning on the inside, helping others, a desperately desired hug, a first kiss, any kiss, morning sunlight, fluffy clouds or blue skies, rainbows, being nude, sunrise, sunset, waterfalls, submerging yourself in refreshing water, being creative, star gazing, butterflies in your tummy, sand in your belly button, dancing in the rain, lying on warm sand, finding Zen and relaxation, a light slumber, stomping in puddles, a great idea, singing loud and terribly with your best friend, afternoon naps and laughing so hard your cheeks hurt!

Try not to take these things for granted.

One day, you'll see these little things are the most important.

Being wealthy is so much more than having money to your name. Abundance is an internal feeling of fullness, not the weight of your wallet.

— How to get rich quick

Thank you for showing up.

Thank you for taking time for yourself, to rest, to play, to challenge your body, mind and soul.

Thank you for listening to your intuition and for respecting your own heart.

Thank you for the warmth you breathe into this world.

Thank you for the happiness you share and the laughter you bring.

Thank you for being kind and welcoming.

Thank you for being able to forgive.

And for being able to move through each new moment with grace and ease.

Thank you for living life fully, despite adversity and with gratitude for all other beings.

Thank you for embracing your truth, your passions and your curiosities.

Thank you for existing wholeheartedly and unapologetically.

I am filled with nothing but expansive and accepting love for you.

And I am excited to feel this love grow as I dance through this life, continually shaping my own reality.

I love who you are, and who you are becoming.

— Letter to myself

If you ever feel down or doubt yourself,

I encourage you to stare deep into your own eyes, and remind

yourself of your courage, resilience and all the countless

times you have risen from the embers.

Over and over again, you will triumph, succeed, prosper and

bloom.

This is where growth happens. This is a place where healing

 happens. A place where I can reflect, withdraw, and retreat to

 any time I need to reconnect.

Sometimes, in order to reach our highest self we must first unfold

 the layers we hide beneath; fear, limiting beliefs, pain,

 insecurities, self-criticism, judgement, comparison.

We need to shed these skins we wear, in order to exist as the

 wholesome light beings we were intended to become.

This is my sanctuary. This is my practice.

If there is one thing I have learnt, it's that growing up means being
    honest.

Honest to others, yes. But mostly to ourselves.

No excuses. No half-truths. No 'tomorrows'. Just ourselves and
    the rawness of our honest reflection.

Be honest about what you want, what you need, what you feel and
    most importantly who you are. It's okay not to be okay. It's
    okay to be flawed and imperfect and it's okay to need help.
    Because at some stage you will be that help to others.

Sometimes change is necessary. But it won't happen unless you
    make it.

The sun is a daily reminder of hope and possibility. It is a daily
reminder that we can rise from the darkness, start over,
begin again.
The sun is a daily reminder of warmth and happiness.
A daily reminder of all the light we can shine upon ourselves and
others.
The sun is a reminder of change and movement; life's constant
flow.
The sun is a daily reminder that nothing begins or ends;
everything simply transforms and shifts.
The sun is a daily reminder of what selfless devotion truly is.
Not once has it received anything in return, yet each day, it
willingly gives.

Ask yourself, 'What is this situation trying to teach me?'

An embraced challenge is an opportunity to grow.

Remember this, and you'll find comfort and reassurance in

the knowledge that everything you experience — good

or bad — is the universe either teaching you something,

helping you to grow, assisting you to learn, grounding you,

strengthening you or using you as a tool to help or teach

someone else.

Everything happens for a reason.

Darling, I wish I could do the hard work for you. I wish I could shift the clouds and blow away the rain. I wish I could kiss your wounds better and wipe the blood from your hands. I wish I could wash away your sins, and make you forget the past. Clear your conscience and make light of this heavy world you wear upon your shoulders. I wish I could take a rainbow and weave it throughout your existence, colour the skies with hope and a little bit of magic. I wish I could heal away the hurt, wrap it up in a warm blanket and carry it as my own. But I can't. I can't, I just can't. This path you're walking must be wandered alone. And as impossible as it may seem, as daunting and scary as it is, I promise you it's worth it. I promise you that you already hold all the strength and courage you will need. I promise you that you will surprise yourself. I promise you that you will find and feel the light you seek.

I promise.

— A letter to my younger self

Every day is a new opportunity for growth and greatness. I'm not waiting until the new year to become a more evolved version of myself. I'm not waiting until next week or even tomorrow. As humans, we have the capacity to shape and reshape our lives in any given moment. And I plan on exercising my right to do so. I'm breaking down my patterns, I'm creating positive shifts, I'm expanding, transforming, maturing, advancing and adapting.

Your healing is your responsibility.

But this does not mean you cannot share your struggles,

or ask for guidance or accept support.

Just because the change is up to you alone,

doesn't mean you need to feel alone.

Hurt is a catalyst for healing.

Wake up and take control of your life.

Have the strength to do what is right, but have the flexibility to do
    it with a smile. Ensure everything you do is bettering you,
    healing you or helping you in some way. Is it bettering,
    helping or healing others too? Do your actions have
    purpose? Can you execute them with intention? Can
    you lighten your footprint? Can you lighten the hearts of
    others? Can you show up, unapologetically? Can you find
    comfort in the unknown? Beauty in the chaos? Can you
    make time to sit in stillness; check in with your physical
    body, mental body, and emotional being?

What can you create? What can you cultivate?

Today is yours for the making.

That's the thing,

You can talk about it all you like.

You can stand on the shore, look out to sea and make plan after
    plan to set sail to liquid infinity.

You can have every intention to remove the sandy earth from
    between your toes, and feel the discomfort of the unfamiliar.

    You can have every intention of growth and transformation.

But talking about it, and actually doing it, are two totally different
    things.

So, ask yourself: are you a talker or an executor?

Repeat after me:

'I am blessed. I have an abundance of energy, courage and
resilience. I am rich in love, kindness and happiness. My life
is fulfilled, and the Universe has provided me with exactly
what I need: elegant sufficiency.

I am happy. I am peaceful. And I am blessed.'

Smiling is like sunshine for your insides.

Dear Universe,

Thank you for blessing me with moments of magic. Thank you for
allowing me to dance and play to the rhythm of my heart.
Thank you for teaching me lessons, and for broadening my
thoughts. Thanks for nurturing my mind, feeding my body
and constantly inspiring my soul.

These are the moments that will soon become the memories we will look back on and smile at sincerely.

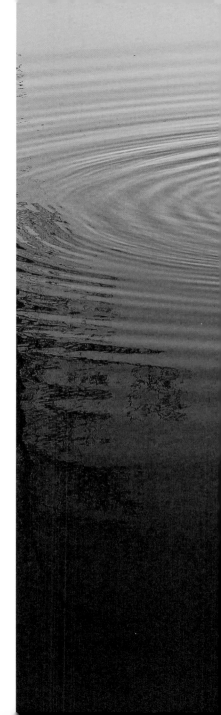

My oh my,

What a miraculous gift it is,

To be suspended on a spiralling planet,

In a mystical universe,

Woven with love,

And sprinkled with magic.

Human is human;

Each of us, just trying to do the best we can, the best way we
    know how.

Constantly evolving, transforming, shifting and growing.

Our constant, is change.

This can be our barrier.

Or it can be our biggest blessing; our birthright.

I am thankful for those who have challenged me, as they aided me

in unearthing my inner power.

These people unwillingly urged me towards my path, and were

essential redirects to my future.

I am thankful for those who have doubted me, as they encouraged

me to find what I believe in and stand firm in my own innate

truth.

These people have earned themselves a front-row seat to my

rebirth and every one of my victories.

I don't see my hardships as a curse.

I see them as blessings;

a fortuitous redirect.

So, I sing and I dance and I pray.

I surrender in divine ecstasy to existence and smile in thanks for

the Great Mother.

It is in her I trust completely.

That tingly feeling.

The one that reminds you that everything will turn out okay.

A slow kiss, an overdue hug, a pleasant surprise, a sunshine

    smooch, fresh rain and wild wind. Salt stains, flower scents,

    chopped grass, sweet berries, new sheets, home cooking

    and him.

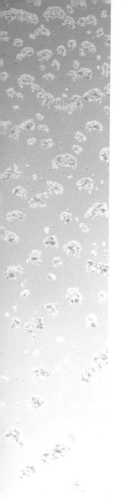

Your healing, begins here.

Finding acknowledgement through the chaos.

Feeling acceptance throughout the excavation of your soul.

Finding grace in space.

Exploring the stillness within movement.

Change is already in progress.

Your growth is inevitable.

Explore
&Transcend

I used to think we had to achieve something to become fulfilled or to do what we came here to do. 'Destiny', if you like.

But I was thinking, what if the purpose of life is really just to feel? To dig deeper, explore, discover, learn, play, develop, grow closer to people/places/things and to just exist and experience as much as we possibly can? Not to 'achieve' anything as such — but just to do things. To intentionally place ourselves outside our comfort zone. To get lost only to find ourselves. To travel the world; see its every corner. To meet new people, fall madly in love with a stranger, taste new foods, try new things, dance under the moon and skinny-dip in secluded, secret places. To switch off, wander solo and listen to what your soul and heart really craves — then go after it! Who says there has to be a 'right' or a 'wrong' way to live?

Just do it, I say. Just go! Have a spoonful of insane courage and start living.

Have no plans, and no intent of ever reaching a destination — knowing that enjoying the journey is the ultimate goal.

This world is
abundant in mystery
and magic.
And we - you and
I - have the privilege
to walk amongst it.

What makes your mind smile?

What brings you joy?

Don't be afraid to be playful, to be quirky and to be silly.

> Cultivate a curiosity for life; explore every emotion, every opportunity, every single moment for everything it is and everything it could be.

This is not your weakness, it is your immense strength.

I used to use travel as a way to escape. I used travel to hide from

my reality. I convinced myself that in order to see beauty,

I needed to cross oceans, hike mountains and discover

new lands.

Now, I don't travel to escape. I travel to explore.

To explore the world, countries, culture, people, psychology,

food, architecture, art and most of all, myself.

Watch the sunset upside down. Do it. Lay on the earth, tilt your head back and allow Mother Nature to leave you speechless in a way you've never experienced.

Notice the way this simple act can transform your entire outlook.

Notice how something simple, mundane and vanilla can become wildly wondrous and truly magnificent. It's like seeing the world through the curious eyes of a child. Everything seems new, everything seems exciting.

· The power of perspective is extraordinary.

I bookmarked this place in my mind, So I can return whenever the skies look grey.

This is it.

This is the air in your lungs, the song that sounds like velvet, the
warmth of a hug and the playful smile of a child. This is the
wagging of a tail, unexpected compliments and those sweet
good-morning kisses.

This is what makes you forget the stress, the anxieties, the troubles.

This is what brings you hope, courage and determination.

This is the moment to live for.

This is it.

Slow down. Enjoy the little things: the process of watching a candle
    burn, making tea, loving oneself, growing a garden, love-
    making, self-grooming, breathing.
Do it all, with the curiosity of a child.
Like it's the first and last time you'll ever see it.

The only thing sweeter than seeing a child at play, is seeing an adult at play with their inner child.

When I'm old, I hope my face is covered in laugh lines and
     wrinkles.

Maps marking the story of my life.

All the giggles, early summer mornings, the sleepless nights spent
     dancing barefoot beneath a sheet of stars, constant jet lag
     and a lifetime of adventure.

I hope they mark my body; I hope I look weathered and worn.

I hope I can wander until my knees buckle and my legs give out.

I hope that every moment of this existence becomes a magnificent
     memory.

I hope I live so fully, so unashamedly and so honestly that there
     is not a single second I would want to change.

A young and ageless soul snuggled inside my creased and
     crinkled frame.

We're complex, we're crazy and we're chaos in motion.

We're capable of complicating even the simplest gesture.

Detectives by nature.

We're divine creatures.

Infinite mysteries.

Our minds follow the waves of our bodies,

Curving to and fro.

The fluidity of the shoreline.

The rise and fall of me.

I am stepping fearlessly into my power and divinity.

Every inhale I take is cleansing.

Every exhale, purifying.

Fall in love with the art of self-love. Slow down, step back, and just breathe.

Take your shoes off and feel the earth beneath your feet. Close your eyes and smile in sweet ecstasy at the feeling of the sun on your skin and the breeze in your hair.

Massage your hands across your body, and give your inner light permission to shine.

Be kind to yourself, be kind to others and be kind to the planet.

Become increasingly aware of your thoughts, actions and their consequences. Become aware of your presence, your innate power and your ability to be the change this world so desperately needs.

Today is the first day of the rest of your life.

You have every opportunity to transform your life. Right now,

make today how you want to live your life.

Choose to take a chance. To make a choice. To make the change

you wish, want or need.

Choose to do all those things you've always wanted to do. I promise

you, that when this is all over, you'll only regret the things

you didn't do.

And sometimes you'll feel like you're sinking, like the world is

trying to swallow you whole.

I promise you, darling — you're fine.

It's simply the ocean wanting you to come back home.

Mother Nature's divine guidance.

A gentle tug of encouragement, asking you to surrender your ego

and allow the Universe to work its wonders.

For you have a larger purpose elsewhere,

A destiny far greater than comprehension.

And when I turned to the moon for direction,

She reminded me that I already knew the way.

This world is beautiful and I've decided I want to experience more of it.

Not by going to more places. But by seeing the places I do go to with fonder eyes and a deeper appreciation for the miracle life is.

Manifest the life you want.

Write letters.

Write forgiveness letters, acceptance letters, write love letters,
write apology letters. Note everything down. Your dreams,
your goals, your fears, your doubts. Write it. Form clear
ideas in your mind of what it is you want in this world, and
then burn the words. Send out to the Universe the things
you are cultivating, challenging or overcoming, and allow
your positive energy to create and develop and alter aspects
of your world. Be open to change. Accept growth wholeheartedly. Embrace the unknown.

Your mere mumblings can have a herculean effect.

It's rare to find the moments where everything is just right.

Where the balance is felt, and neutral is in sight.

The moments between the here and there.

The space between the head and heart.

Not yet the end, nor at the start.

309

Your beliefs can be beautiful.

But your beliefs can also be your boundaries.

So explore, endlessly.

Allow your curiosity to guide you.

Acknowledge your truth — the truth you know from learned
experience — but allow room for challenge, change and
transformation.

Find and feel the freedom of non-attachment.

There is only oneness, between all of us. Despite all of our differences.

I watched the sun rise above me.

I pulled up, parked myself upon a ledge, and watched in awe as the

sky unfolded.

An array of pastels,

Burning like flamingo feathers on fire.

There is an exquisite mystery in the morning sky; knowing the

world is so much greater than you and allowing this to

belittle your problems.

How beautiful it is,

to allow the Divine to work through you,

and know that the Universe supports you.

Here's to being silly.

Here's to having fun, bursting into uncontrollable fits of laughter
and smiling so wide your cheeks hurt.

Here's to playfulness.

Here's to freedom.

And here's to an open mind and heart.

Here's to the dreamers, the doers, the believers.

Here's to the slightly weird, ridiculously wonderful humans
who practise what it truly means to enjoy the moment and
appreciate life.

Here's to those wild enough to embody what it truly means to live
rather than just survive.

Here's to pulling faces, making up words, indulging in secret
handshakes and viewing the world with wonder.

Here's to the five-year-old child within each and every one of us.

Today I will practise presence. I will enjoy the place where
life happens. I will take each moment, and embrace it
wholeheartedly. I will share my energy with the Universe,
and it will share its energy with me. Together, we will create
a day of gratitude, grace and countless tiny victories.

Your reality is a direct reflection of your mindset. What you get, is what and *how* you think. Understand this, and you will begin to understand that you have the greatest power and authority over your own life.

'The best poem I will ever write, is the one that I will live.'

— No pen required

Acknowledgements

To those who have loved me, I say thank you.

To those who have hurt me, I say thank you.

To those who have helped heal me, I say thank you.

To those who have challenged me, I say thank you.

To anyone and everyone, anything and everything that has ever confronted me,
supported me, frustrated me, bent me or broken me, I say
THANK YOU.

Thank you for your impact. Thank you for your presence. Thank you for your existence.

Thank you for outlining my strengths and reflecting my vulnerabilities.

Thank you for teaching me patience, and helping me to practise acceptance and
unconditional forgiveness.

Thank you for forcing me to evolve, over and over. Constant rebirth, constant growth.

Thank you for the pivotal role you have performed throughout the process of this human
experience.

It is because of you, I have learned the lessons that lace this book.

It is because of you, I know my truth.

And it is because of you, I will continue to explore the limitations of this incarnation.

For YOU, I am eternally grateful.

Special shout out to my mum, Judy.

You refused to give up on me, even when I gave up on myself.

I know I can be hard to love sometimes, but that never stopped you.

One day I hope I can be half as good of a mother as you are.

To my dad, Michael, and two brothers, Josh and Sam, for constantly reminding me of my worth, and protecting me unconditionally. For being my rocks. (And for always knowing how to fix the things I break! Seriously though?! Is there anything you guys can't do!?)

To my past lovers, thank you for releasing me.

I didn't know it at the time, but you were direct redirects to my destined evolution.

You taught me the resilience of the human heart.

To my former self, thank you, I see you and I forgive you.

Every time you bent beneath the weight of this world, you created a catalyst for expansion, and rebirth.

To my current self, thank you for your faith and for choosing to remain soft.

To my future self, thank you for your patience.

Hold on girl, you got this.

And lastly, to YOU. The beautiful reader. To the one who is cradling this book in your palms.

Thank you for opening your heart, for your support, for sharing your time and energy with me in these pages.

This book has been just as healing for me to write, as I hope it was for you to read.

EBURY PRESS

UK | USA | Canada | Ireland | Australia
India | New Zealand | South Africa | China

Ebury Press is part of the Penguin Random House group of companies
whose addresses can be found at global.penguinrandomhouse.com.

Penguin
Random House
Australia

First published by Ebury Press, 2020

Cover photograph by Louis Solywoda

Cover design, internal design and typesetting by Louisa Maggio © Penguin Random House Australia

Printed and bound by 1010 Printing

 A catalogue record for this
book is available from the
National Library of Australia

ISBN 978 1 76089 786 4

penguin.com.au